EASIEST KEYBOARD COLLECTION

Chart Busters!

WISE PUBLICATIONS
part of The Music Sales Group
London/New York/Paris/Sydney/Copenhagen/Berlin/Madrid/Tokyo

Published by
Wise Publications
8/9 Frith Street,
London W1D 3JB, England.

Exclusive Distributors:
Music Sales Limited
Distribution Centre, Newmarket Road,
Bury St Edmunds, Suffolk, IP33 3YB, England.
Music Sales Pty Limited
120 Rothschild Avenue,
Rosebery, NSW 2018,
Australia.

Order No. AM985105
ISBN 1-84609-461-5
This book © Copyright 2006 by Wise Publications
a division of Music Sales Limited.

Compiled by Nick Crispin.
Music arranged by Vasco Hexel.
Music processed by Paul Ewers Music Design.

Printed in the United Kingdom by
Caligraving Limited, Thetford, Norfolk.

Your Guarantee of Quality
As publishers, we strive to produce every book to the highest
commercial standards.
The music has been freshly engraved and the book has been carefully
designed to minimise awkward page turns and to make playing from
it a real pleasure.
Particular care has been given to specifying acid-free, neutral-sized
paper made from pulps which have not been elemental chlorine
bleached. This pulp is from farmed sustainable forests and was
produced with special regard for the environment.
Throughout, the printing and binding have been planned to ensure
a sturdy, attractive publication which should give years of enjoyment.
If your copy fails to meet our high standards, please inform us and
we will gladly replace it.

www.musicsales.com

Contents

ALL TIME LOVE

Words & Music by Jamie Hartman

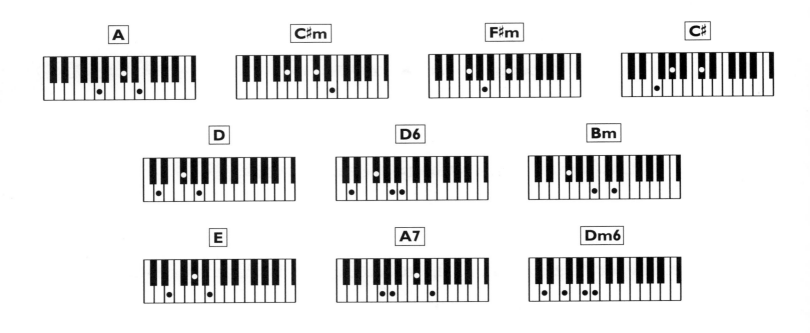

Voice: **Alto Saxophone**

Rhythm: **Rock Ballad**

Tempo: ♩ = 75

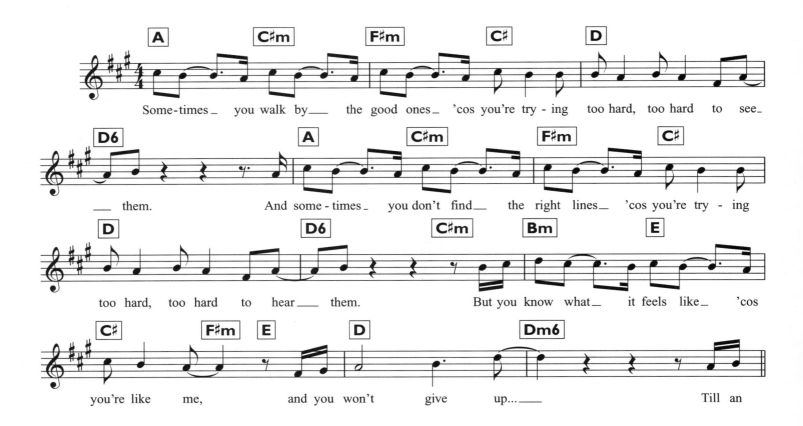

Some-times___ you walk by___ the good ones___ 'cos you're try - ing too hard, too hard to see___

___ them. And some - times___ you don't find___ the right lines___ 'cos you're try - ing

too hard, too hard to hear___ them. But you know what___ it feels like___ 'cos

you're like me, and you won't give up... ___ Till an

ARMY OF LOVERS

Words & Music by Nigel Hoyle

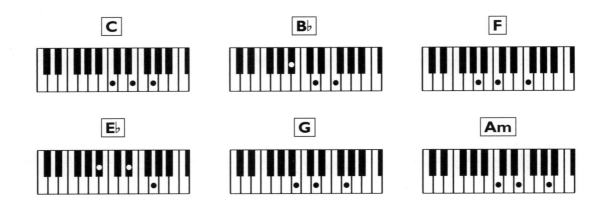

Voice: **Flute**

Rhythm: **Rock Ballad**

Tempo: ♩ = 78

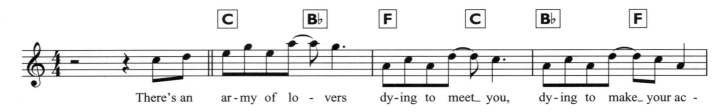

There's an ar-my of lo-vers dy-ing to meet_ you, dy-ing to make_ your ac-

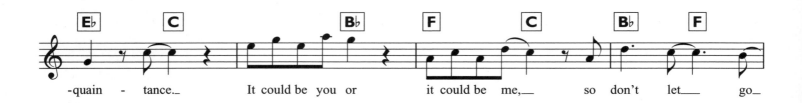

-quain - tance._ It could be you or it could be me,_ so don't let_ go_

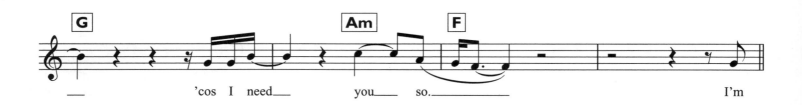

_ 'cos I need_ you_ so._ I'm

yours and you are_ mine,_ there's some-thing a - bout_

BECAUSE OF YOU

Words & Music by Kelly Clarkson, Ben Moody & David Hodges

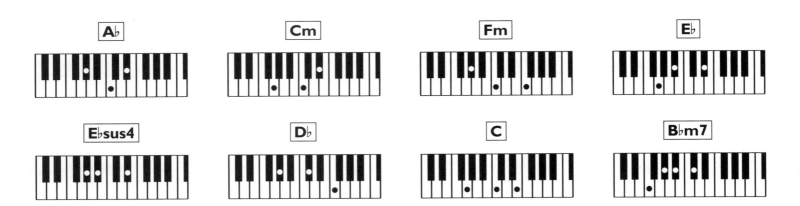

Voice: **Alto Saxophone**

Rhythm: **Rock Ballad**

Tempo: ♩ = 70

CALL MY NAME

Words & Music by Charlotte Church, Wayne Hector & Francis White

Voice: **Fat Synth**

Rhythm: **Electro Pop**

Tempo: ♩ = 120

DAKOTA

Words & Music by Kelly Jones

DON'T CHA

Words & Music by Thomas Callaway & Anthony Ray

DO YOU WANT TO

Words & Music by Alexander Kapranos, Nicholas McCarthy, Robert Hardy & Paul Thomson

Voice: **Electric Guitar**

Rhythm: **Straight Rock**

Tempo: ♩ = 130

Oh, well, I woke up to-night and said I'm _____ gon-na make some-bo-dy love _____

_____ me, I'm gon-na make some-bo-dy love _____ me And now I know, now I know, now I

know, I know it is you. _____ You're luck-y, luck-y, you're so luck-y! _____ (Do, do, do,

do, do, do, do, do. Do, do, do, do, do, do, do, do. Do, do, do, do, do, do, do, do.)

Well, do you, do _____ you, do you want to? Well, do you, do _____ you, do you want to, want to

FIX YOU

Words & Music by Guy Berryman, Chris Martin, Jon Buckland & Will Champion

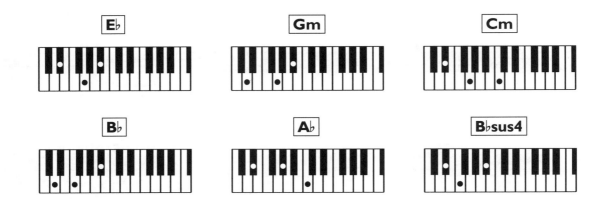

Voice: **Rock Organ**

Rhythm: **Soft Rock 2**

Tempo: ♩ = **70**

When you try your best but you don't suc-ceed.___ When you

get what you want but not what you need.___ When you

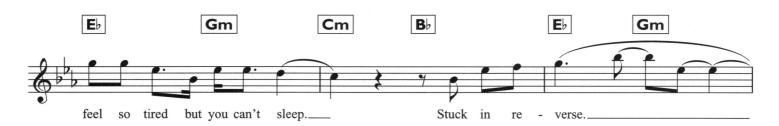

feel so tired but you can't sleep.___ Stuck in re-verse.___

___ And the tears___ come stream-ing down your face___ when you

HUNG UP

Words & Music by Benny Andersson, Bjorn Ulvaeus, Madonna & Stuart Price

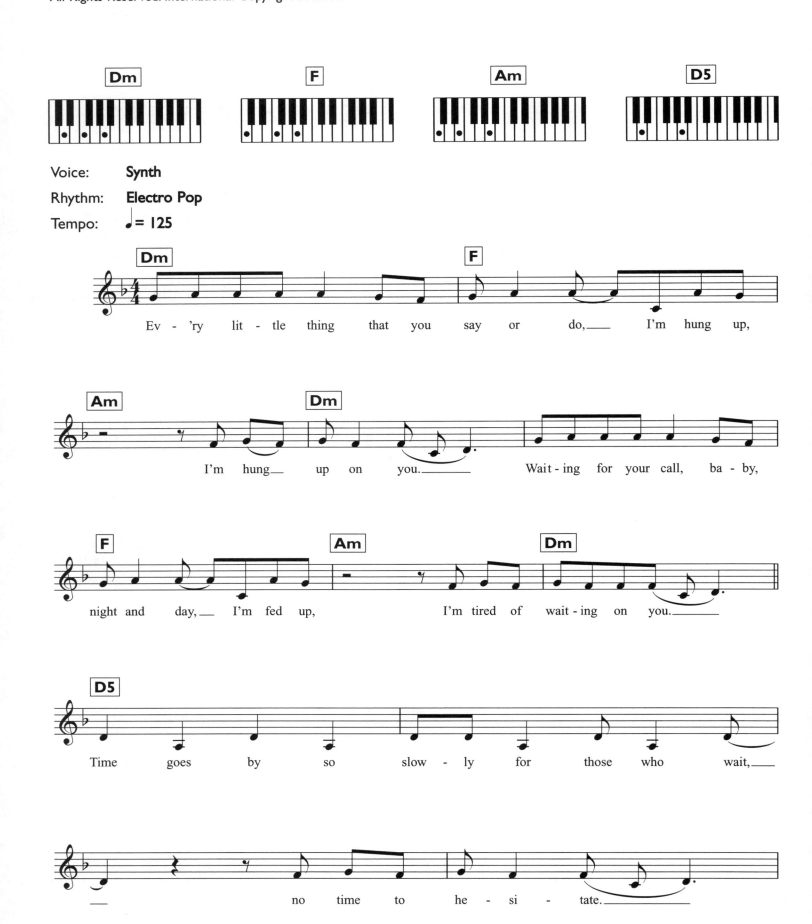

Those who run seem to have all the fun,___ I'm caught up,___

___ I don't know what to do.___

Time goes by so slow - ly. Time goes by so slow - ly.

Time goes by so slow - ly, I don't know what to do.___

Dm ... **F**

Ev - 'ry lit - tle thing that you say or do,___ I'm hung up,

Am ... **Dm**

I'm hung___ up on you.___ Wait - ing for your call, ba - by,

F ... **Am** ... **Dm** ... *Repeat to fade*

night and day,___ I'm fed up, I'm tired of wait - ing on you.___

I PREDICT A RIOT

Words & Music by Nicholas Hodgson, Richard Wilson, Andrew White, James Rix & Nicholas Baines

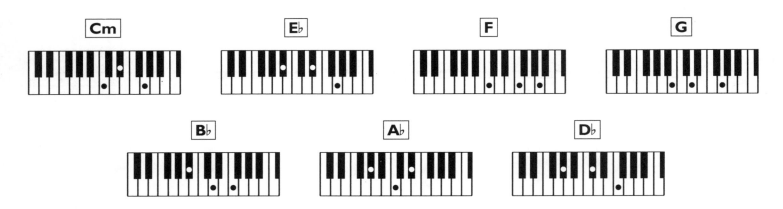

Voice: **Electric Guitar**

Rhythm: **Hard Rock**

Tempo: ♩ = 158

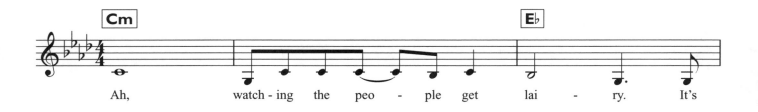

Ah, watch - ing the peo - ple get lai - ry. It's

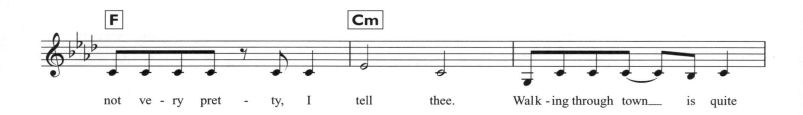

not ve - ry pret - ty, I tell thee. Walk - ing through town___ is quite

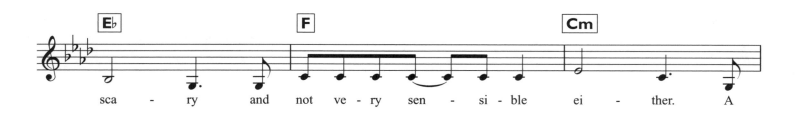

sca - ry and not ve - ry sen - si - ble ei - ther. A

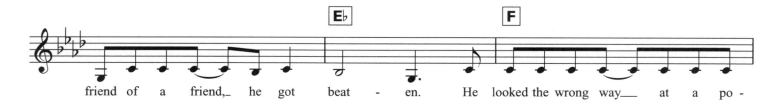

friend of a friend,___ he got beat - en. He looked the wrong way___ at a po -

-lice - man. Would ne - ver have hap - pened to Smea - ton, an

old Le - o - den - si - an. La - ah - ah,

la - la - la - la - la - la. Ah - ah - ah, la -

- la, la - la - la - la - la - la._____

I pre - dict a ri - ot, I_____ pre - dict a

ri - ot. I pre - dict a ri - ot,

I_____ pre - dict a ri - ot.

I WANNA HOLD YOU

Words & Music by Thomas Fletcher, Daniel Jones & Dougie Poynter
© Copyright 2005 Universal Music Publishing Limited.
All Rights Reserved. International Copyright Secured.

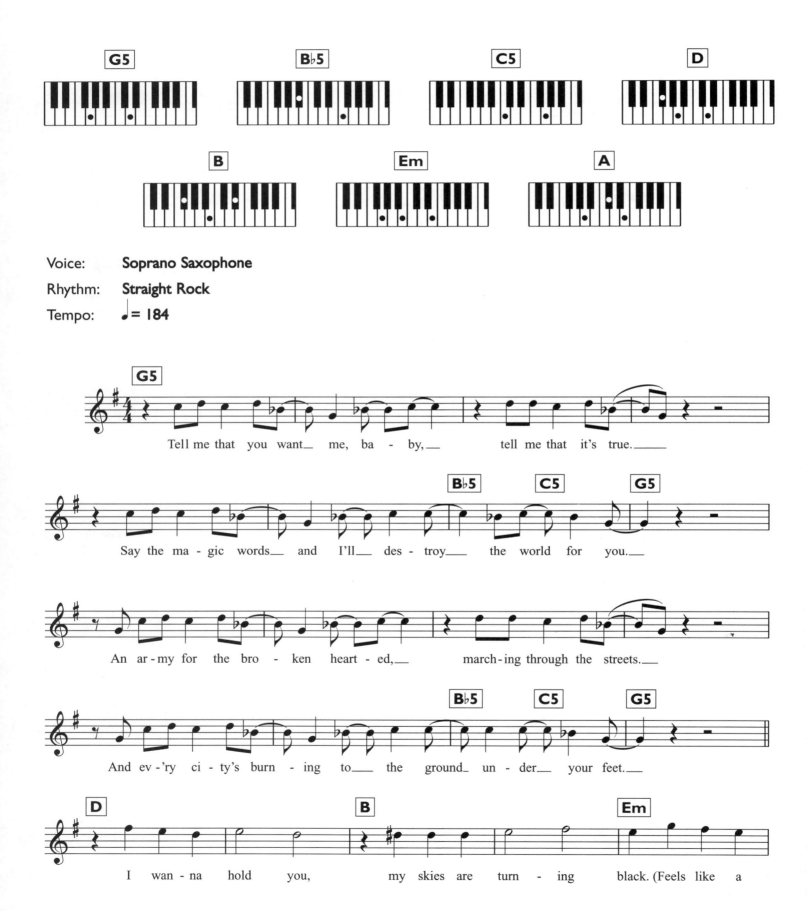

Voice: **Soprano Saxophone**

Rhythm: **Straight Rock**

Tempo: ♩ = 184

Tell me that you want me, ba - by, tell me that it's true.

Say the ma - gic words and I'll des - troy the world for you.

An ar - my for the bro - ken heart - ed, march - ing through the streets.

And ev - 'ry ci - ty's burn - ing to the ground un - der your feet.

I wan - na hold you, my skies are turn - ing black. (Feels like a

LET THERE BE LOVE

Words & Music by Noel Gallagher

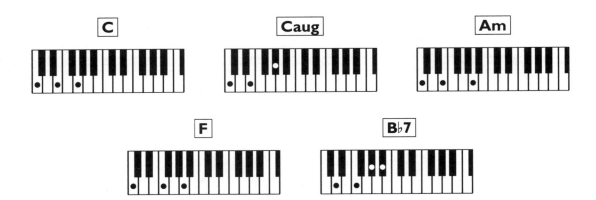

Voice: Alto Saxophone

Rhythm: Rock Ballad

Tempo: ♩ = 75

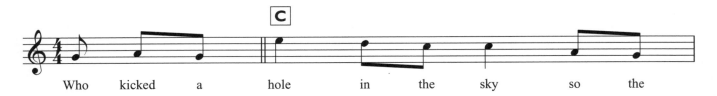

Who kicked a hole in the sky so the

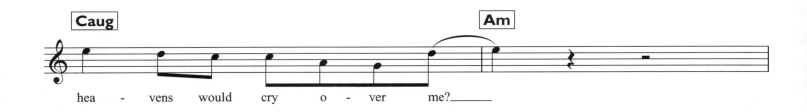

hea - vens would cry o - ver me?_____

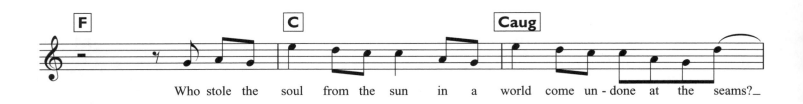

Who stole the soul from the sun in a world come un - done at the seams?_____

_ Let there be love._____

NO WORRIES

Words & Music by Matthew Prime & Timothy Woodcock

THE ONE I LOVE

Words & Music by David Gray & Craig McClune

PUSH THE BUTTON

Words & Music by Dallas Austin, Mutya Buena, Heidi Range & Kiesha Buchanan

Voice: **Alto Saxophone**

Rhythm: **Electro Pop**

Tempo: ♩ = 120

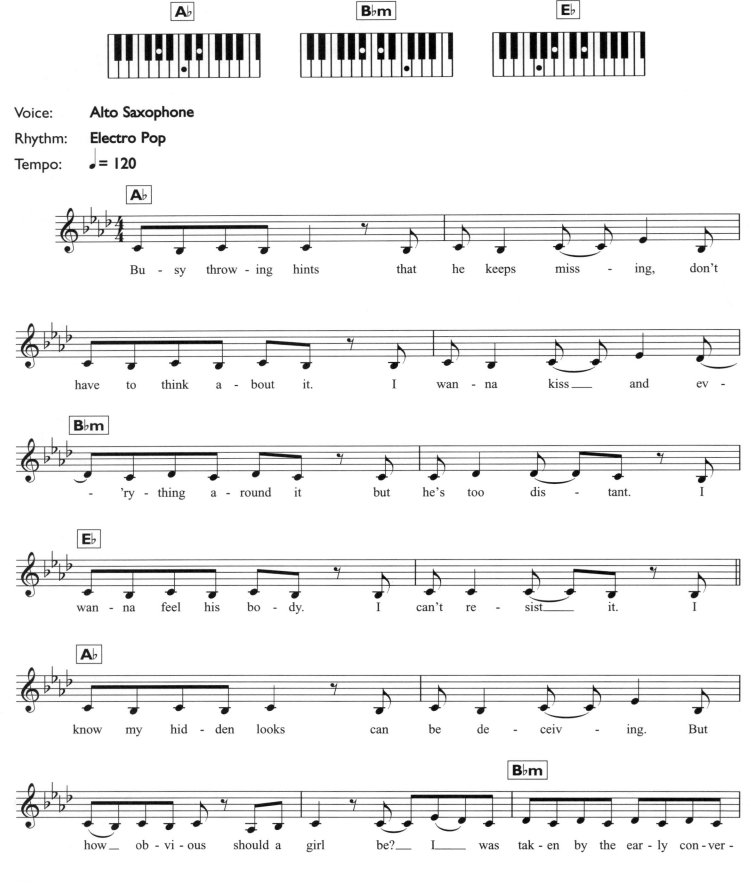

-sa - tion piece_ and I real - ly like the way that he res - pec - ted me._

I've been wait - ing pa - tient - ly for him to come and get it, I

won - der if he knows that he can say it and I'm with it. I knew I had my mind made up from

the ve - ry be - gin - ning. Catch this op - por - tu - ni - ty so you and me could feel it 'cos...

If you're rea - dy for me boy __ you'd bet - ter

push the but - ton and let me know be - fore I get the wrong i - dea

and go,_ you're gon - na miss the freak that I con - trol._

33

RIDE A WHITE HORSE

Words & Music by William Gregory, Nicholas Batt & Alison Goldfrapp

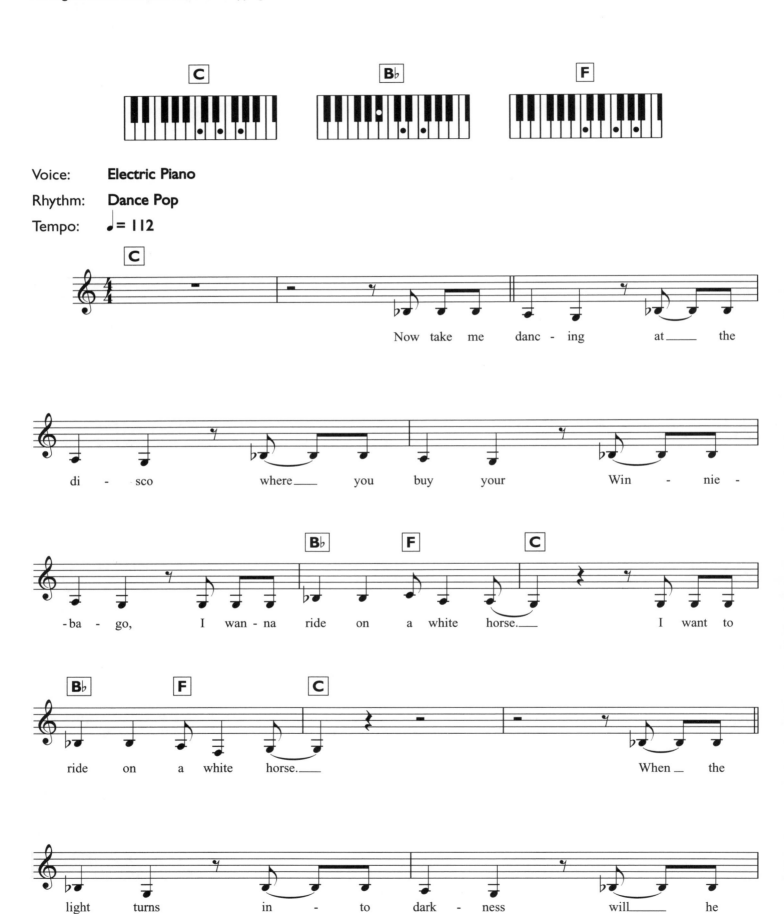

turn up to___ ex - plain us? I wan - na ride on a white horse.___

___ I want to ride on a white horse.___

Lend me a whole___ new world___ all

night,___ feel life.___

Oh, oh.___

When is there ev - er sense___ to love___ this

world?___ Oh, oh.___

SONG 4 LOVERS

Words & Music by Joseph Simmons, Tom Lundon, Grant Black, Benedetto Di Massa, Marlene Buck & Garry Wilson

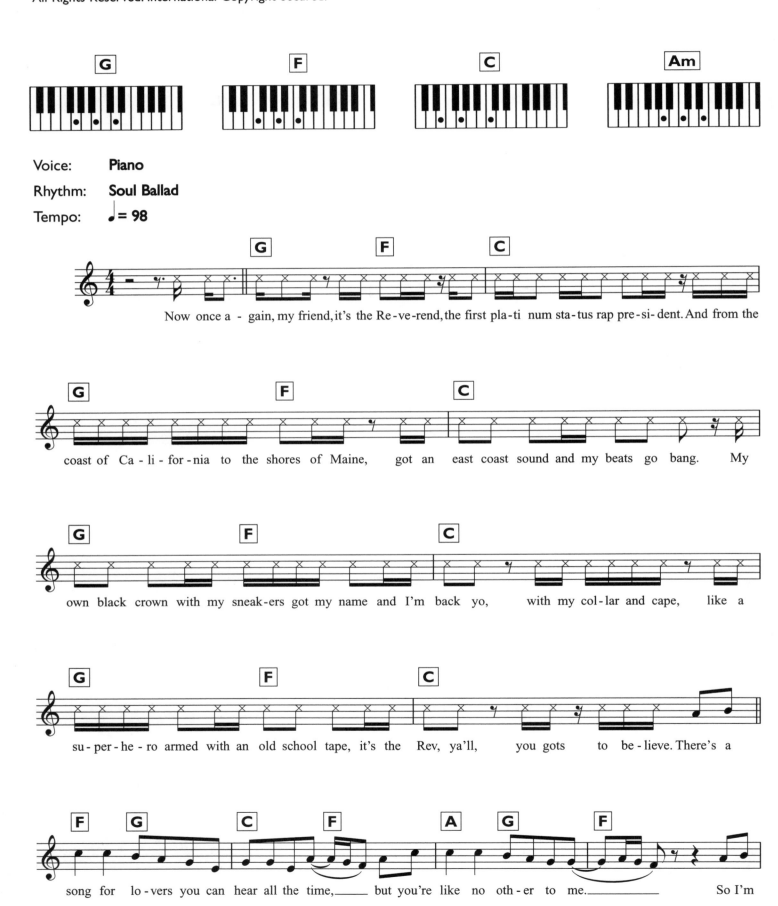

not gon-na pro-mise you a star-ry sky,_____ you just need to be-lieve._____ I take

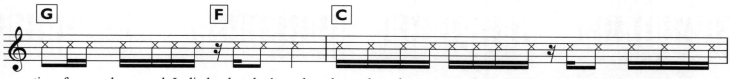

time for my rhyme and I climb but don't reach, hus-tle when we rus-tle and grime and rock beats. And this is

it, what? An-oth-er hit for the streets, I got love for my peo-ple from Queens to o-ver-seas.

Step in-to the room and then "Boom!" The horns scream. Rev's com-ing well and re-gal, I've got dreams.

Just like Mar-tin Lu-ther the King, I might teach. Rock a col-lar to the par-ty af-ter par-ty goin' preach. There's a

song for lo-vers you can hear all the time,_____ but you're like no oth-er to me._____ So I'm

not gon-na pro-mise you a star-ry sky,_____ you just need to be-lieve._____

SUDDENLY I SEE

Words & Music by KT Tunstall

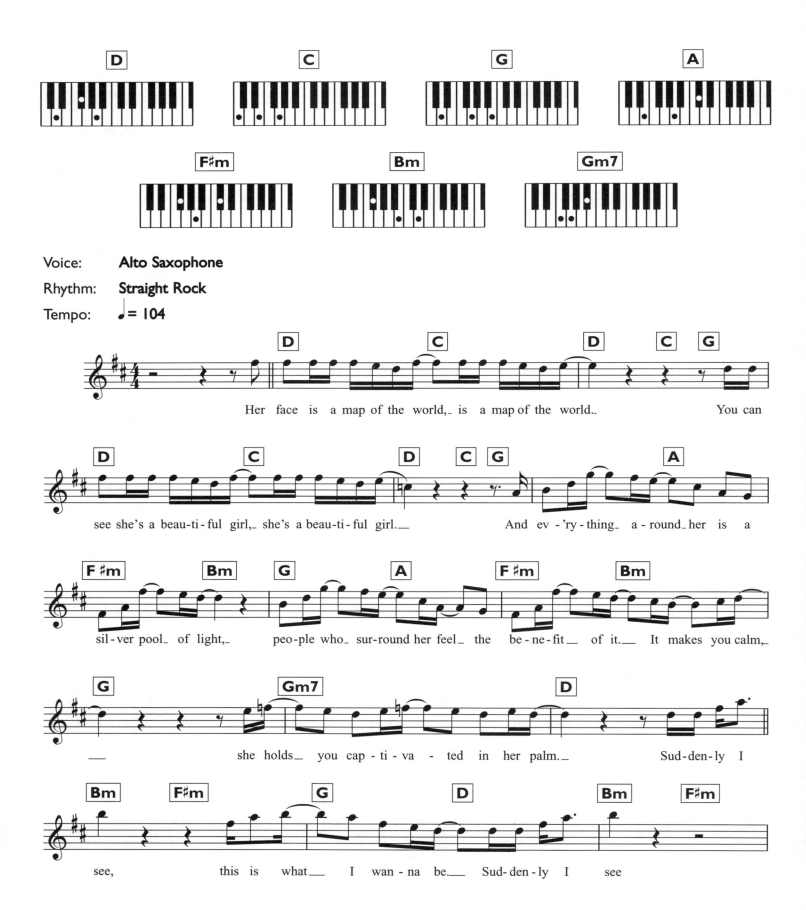

Voice: **Alto Saxophone**

Rhythm: **Straight Rock**

Tempo: ♩ = 104

THAT'S MY GOAL

Words & Music by Jörgen Elofsson, Bill Padley & Jeremy Godfrey

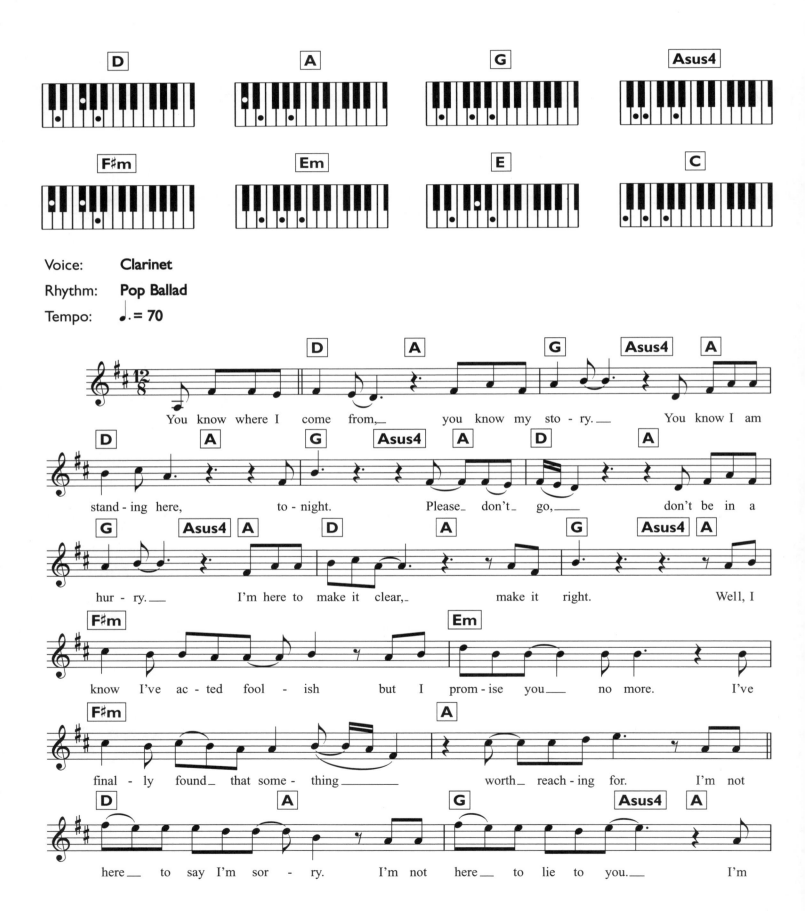

TRIPPIN'

Words & Music by Robbie Williams & Stephen Duffy

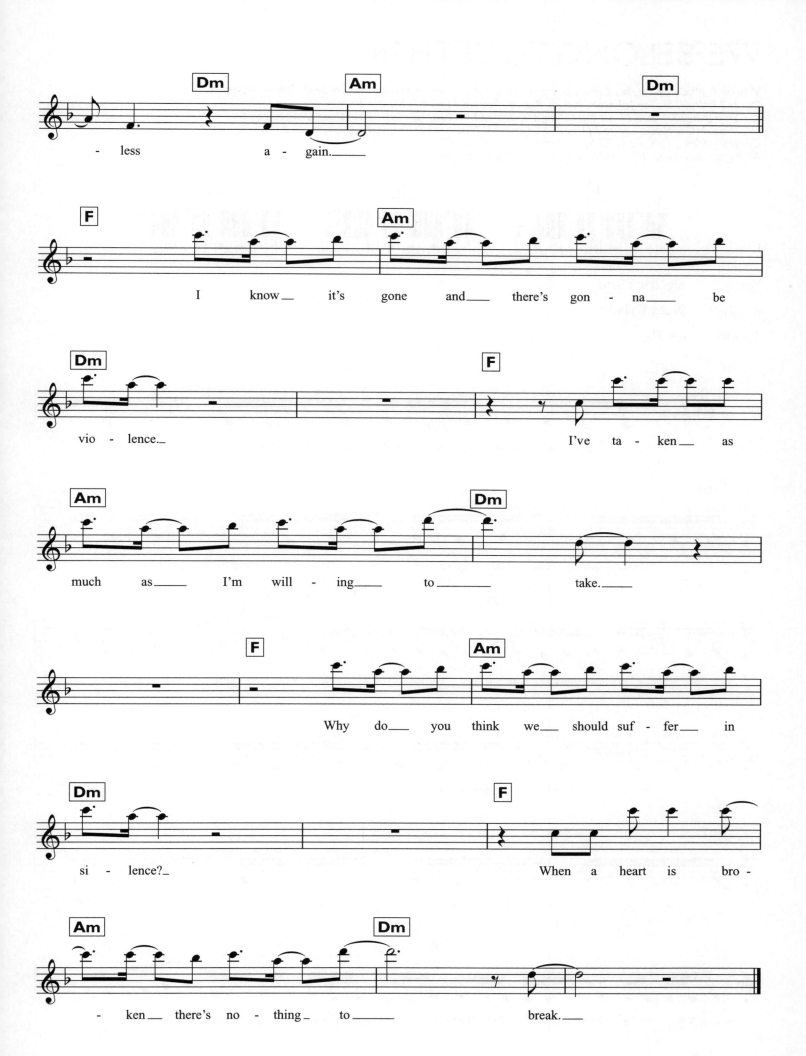

WE BELONG TOGETHER

Words & Music by Mariah Carey, Jermaine Dupri, Kenneth Edmonds, Manuel Seal, Bobby Womack, Darnell Bristol, Sidney Johnson, Johnta Austin, Patrick Moten & Sandra Sully

Voice: **Electric Piano**

Rhythm: **Blues Ballad**

Tempo: ♩ = 70

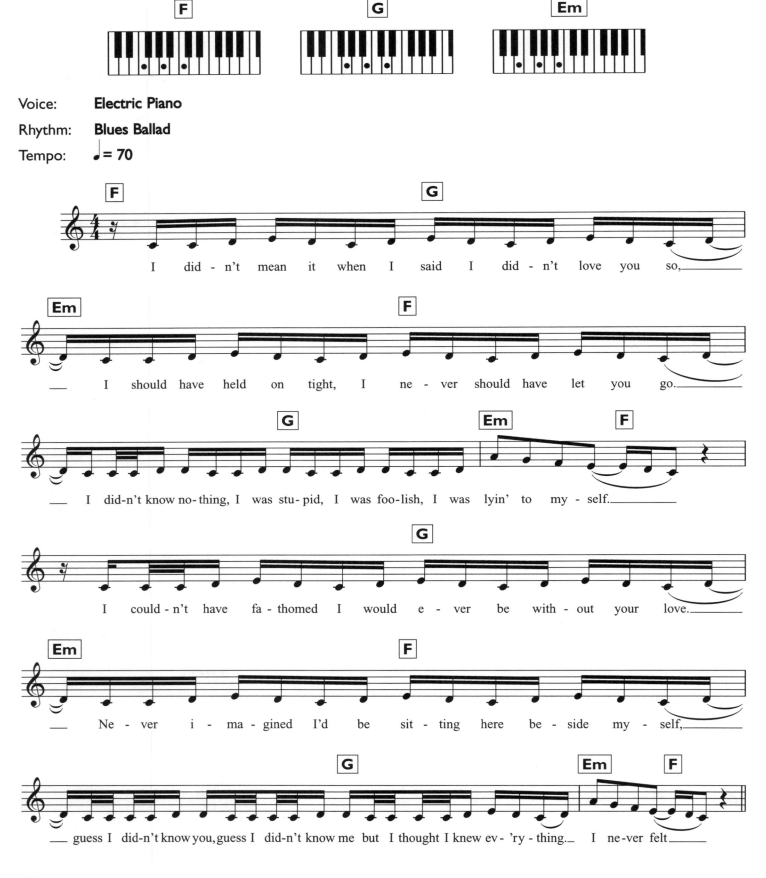

the feel - ing that I'm feel - ing now that I don't hear your voice

or have your touch and kiss your lips, 'cos I don't have a choice.

Oh, what I would-n't give to have you ly - ing by my side, right here, 'cos ba - by,

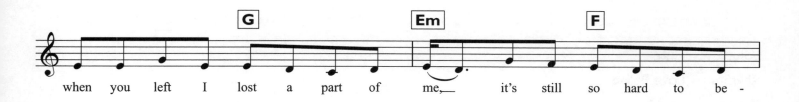

when you left I lost a part of me,___ it's still so hard to be -

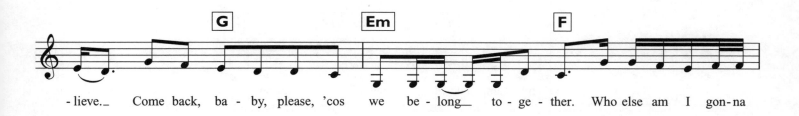

- lieve.__ Come back, ba - by, please, 'cos we be - long___ to - ge - ther. Who else am I gon-na

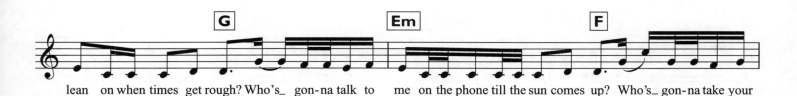

lean on when times get rough? Who's_ gon-na talk to me on the phone till the sun comes up? Who's_ gon-na take your

place? There ain't no - bo - dy bet - ter, oh, ba - by, ba - by, we be - long___ to - ge - ther.

YOU RAISE ME UP

Words & Music by Rolf Lovland & Brendan Graham

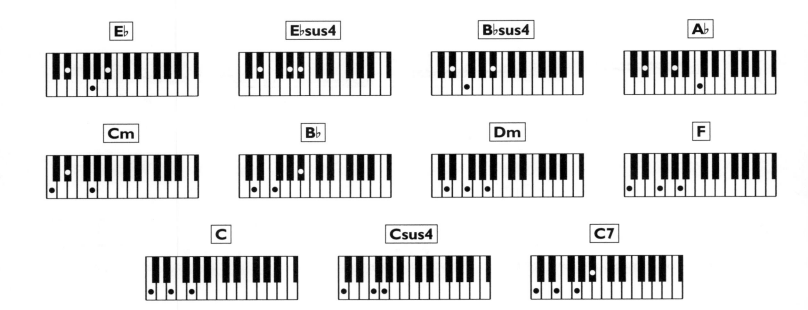

Voice: **Flute**

Rhythm: **Love Ballad**

Tempo: ♩ = 60

When I am down and, oh, my soul, so wea - ry. When trou - bles

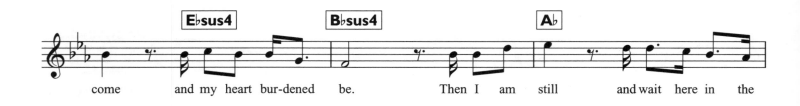

come and my heart bur - dened be. Then I am still and wait here in the

si - lence un - til you come and sit a - while with me. You raise me

EASIEST KEYBOARD COLLECTION

Easy-to-play melody line arrangements for all keyboards with chord symbols and lyrics. Suggested registration, rhythm and tempo are included for each song together with keyboard diagrams showing left-hand chord voicings used.

 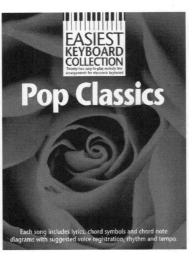 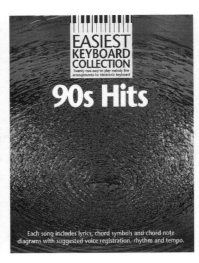 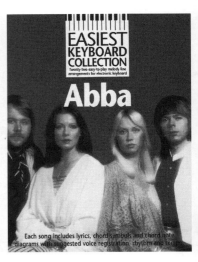

Showstoppers
Consider Yourself (Oliver!), Do You Hear The People Sing? (Les Misérables), I Know Him So Well (Chess), Maria (West Side Story), Smoke Gets In Your Eyes (Roberta) and 17 more big stage hits.
Order No. AM944218

Pop Classics
A Whiter Shade Of Pale (Procol Harum), Bridge Over Troubled Water (Simon & Garfunkel), Crocodile Rock (Elton John) and 19 more classic hit songs, including Hey Jude (The Beatles), Imagine (John Lennon), and Massachusetts (The Bee Gees).
Order No. AM944196

90s Hits
Over 20 of the greatest hits of the 1990s, including Always (Bon Jovi), Fields Of Gold (Sting), Have I Told You Lately (Rod Stewart), One Sweet Day (Mariah Carey), Say You'll Be There (Spice Girls), and Wonderwall (Oasis).
Order No. AM944229

Abba
A great collection of 22 Abba hit songs. Includes: Dancing Queen, Fernando, I Have A Dream, Mamma Mia, Super Trouper, Take A Chance On Me, Thank You For The Music, The Winner Takes It All, and Waterloo.
Order No. AM959860

Also available...

Ballads, Order No. AM952116	**The Corrs,** Order No. AM959849
The Beatles, Order No. NO90686	**Elton John,** Order No. AM958320
Boyzone, Order No. AM958331	**Film Themes,** Order No. AM952050
Broadway, Order No. AM952127	**Hits of the 90s,** Order No. AM955780
Celine Dion, Order No. AM959850	**Jazz Classics,** Order No. AM952061
Chart Hits, Order No. AM952083	**Love Songs,** Order No. AM950708
Christmas, Order No. AM952105	**Pop Hits,** Order No. AM952072
Classic Blues, Order No. AM950697	**60s Hits,** Order No. AM955768
Classics, Order No. AM952094	**80s Hits,** Order No. AM955779

...plus many more!